Uz Hardwick

Learning to Have Lost

Oz Hardwick

Learning to Have Lost

IPSI CHAPBOOK 13

University of Canberra
International Poetry Studies Institute
Series editor: Paul Munden

RECENT
WORK
PRESS

Learning to Have Lost
Second edition
IPSI with Recent Work Press
Canberra, Australia

ISBN: 9780648553748 (paperback)

First published 2018
International Poetry Studies Institute
Faculty of Arts and Design
University of Canberra
Canberra, Australia
http://ipsi.org.au

Design by Caren Florance

Contents

Unwrapping   1
Graduation   2
Interplanetary   3
The Universal Petting Zoo   4
Name Tags   5
Station . . .   6
Noir   7
Bluff   8
An Alternative Wedding Album   9
Theology: A Short Introduction   10
Crafts for the Home   11
Origami   12
Half a Century   13
The Do-It-Yourself Horror Movie   14
Space Invaders   15
DIY for the Unconvinced   16
When He Leaves   17
Au   18
In a Stranger's Car   19
Highway Code: Addendum   20
Jazz   21
The Beast from the East   22
. . . to Station   23
Cats' Eyes   24
At the Late-Night Pharmacy   25
Wrapping   26

Unwrapping

And when they lift these white cloths from around your shoulders, you may not feel the lightness of release, but will know that a window has opened, letting out the dust. You will know that music has stopped – or started – in that ballroom where you once sat aside on a high chair, your feet not touching the ground. You will know that the spring tide – which, as you told me years ago, has nothing to do with the season – has passed the mark you scratched on the wall. You will know that a grey cat sleeps before the fire in the house where you were born. And when you feel the itch of white wings beneath your skin, you will understand why.

Graduation

On the last day, he never even emptied his schoolbag; just threw it in the cupboard in the spare room with carrier bags full of letters, photographs and pressed flowers. He moved out of the family home, acquired a job and a drink problem, a successful business and an unsuccessful marriage. He wouldn't think about it for years, but three or four times he had a dream in which he found it, still where he'd left it, opened it up, and wept at what was inside, though he could never remember what it was when he woke up. Then once, when he was visiting his now aged parents, he had an urge to look, and there it was, still. With pre-emptive tears prickling his eyes, he opened it and saw that the books had grown back into trees, with damp grass all around, and there were birds like notes on telegraph wires, singing a song he'd written in an abandoned bandstand: it was about cheap sparkling cider, the smell of fireworks, subtle indentations in a sloping lawn.

Interplanetary

Weightless, she watches Earth, the way a fox watches chickens, the way a watch tells hours. Messages from home gather like satellites, patterning space, sending weak but incessant signals, just off the dial. Each day I gather reminders, press them into tight pills to be swallowed like science fiction, flip them high for her to catch like a performing seal, muscling from its native element. It's more Jules Verne than Neil Armstrong, but paper is stronger than Avcoat, and burns brighter. Each day brings new breakthroughs, and there have been so many miracles that we've stopped counting, but some certainties remain: the universe is expanding, all things end, and the smell of mothballs will always remind me of my grandmother.

The Universal Petting Zoo

Each time she returns from feeding the animals, she is smaller, adhering to processes more familiar in astronomy. We both know the universe is expanding, but deal with it in different ways: I measure the lapses between echoes, the volume of traffic on the Great North Road; she collects furniture for dolls' houses that were demolished after the war. There are still trains running to the coast, though there are more stations now that it's getting further, in inverse proportion to the sea's greedy consumption of the land. If we could map it out, it would be a Moebius strip, looping back and forth through time and space, patterned with words we let drop, smudged at the places where we almost touched.

Name Tags

The last thing she does is sew name tags into every item of clothing: clumsy stitches, but strong, each stitch a year, linking back to her children. Their school's now a surgery, the playground a carpark, her fingers dry sticks, awkward with sharp steel. But her daughter's in her old bedroom, blow-drying her hair and singing, her son's cutting neat sandwiches, there are bright rings on next month's calendar, and there are taxis queueing at the door. Soon they will all depart, these scattered clothes the only things still bearing names.

Station . . .

Time was, I'd fall asleep on trains, wake up with a hangover to find myself three, four, ten towns beyond my destination. I'd arrive home hours late, unsure where I'd been. After a time, I started waking up in strange houses; sometimes on a sofa, sometimes in a bed, once in a large, white room full of silence and flowers. It was a knack I had. Now, I rarely wake up at all, sleeping across whole countries as strangers try to ignore me, bustling about their days. A friend thought she once saw me nodding through smeared railway glass in a flat West Country summer, but neither of us could be sure.

Noir

It's the shadow on the empty street, the movement at the periphery on the tired night journey. I've been up 36 hours straight, maybe longer. Or perhaps the noise, or the movement, or the headlines, or just the pills, have crumbled sleep into untidy fragments that don't fit together into anything. Either way, I see – or think I see, and what's the difference? – a nearly-shape just long enough to make another papercut in my disjunction, that will suddenly sting when I've almost forgotten it. It makes no sense, but I know it's coming for me.

Bluff

I've forgotten the rules to the card games we played, but remember how we'd sit, serious as movies, studying our awkward hands. We smoked the roots of those flowers from the river, then soothed our throats with chilled cider. It did the trick, and we shared a sleeping-bag in the damp back bedroom, listening to the sea. I sometimes think that there weren't any rules, though there must have been, or I couldn't have lost.

An Alternative Wedding Album

I have never understood colour: its proclivities and insinuations. If the bride wants to wear green, that's a matter for her own conscience, and no posse of well-wishers has the right to drown her, witch or not. It's the same with uniforms: as long as the ties point sharply to the floor and the shoes shine like poison berries, they could be black, beige or proverbial purple, for all it matters, socks notwithstanding. What's in the blood stays in the blood, and what's under the skin can't be changed, yet the silks you choose for your white ankles apparently make all the difference, and all your seductive curses are taken down in red ink.

Theology: A Short Introduction

Marble wings beat slower than mercury, as marble hearts beat slower than grass: this is the essence of angels. Sometimes you suspect theology is just a matter of simple equations, and that maybe the answers are at the back, but when you turn to the end you find nothing but blank pages where the narrator ran out of ideas. Afterwards, when you flick through to find your place, all the words are in Aramaic – or at least in emojis you haven't encountered before. In spite of this, exegesis remains a matter for muscle memory, like the ache in your jaws when you slip into your native accent, or the way you catch an apple falling from the sky. Yet, when the divine messengers call your name, and when you follow their words back to what you assume to be their quicksilver source, all you find is a mouth sprouting grass, carved feathers, and a marble heart so slow that it has forgotten blood.

Crafts for the Home

For a year or so in the '60s, every home had at least one jar covered in shells pressed into putty by their kids' thumbs. Some were vases – ours held pencils. I don't remember the last time I sharpened a pencil but, though it's too late for Christmas and it's not my birthday, you give me a pencil sharpener shaped like a fox. I'll pin it to the wall, like the most famous work in a gallery; sell reproductions and postcards to queues of tourists; print a leaflet on its provenance. And tonight I'll sculpt a gift for you: my empty ribcage studded with stars – Nu Octanis, Sima Octanis. It'll hold umbrellas for a year or so, then vanish who knows where.

Origami

As you fold the sheets, it reminds me of the Great Origami Craze of '68-'69. Wherever you went, there were people folding squares into something-or-other: frogs that hopped when you tapped them with a pencil, lotuses that opened to reveal Shiva, delicately balanced and winking. Some days, the air was so thick with planes that you had to fold bell-like umbrellas to keep their sharp noses at bay. On rainy days, gutters would become armadas of frigates and galleons, each bristling with guns that pinged matchsticks off passing traffic. Origami was prime time entertainment, there were special live broadcasts at breakfast time from the world championships in Mexico City, and soaps would end on a seemingly impossible crease, leaving the nation anxiously awaiting the outcome the following evening. A surgeon won the Nobel Prize for the first successful origami heart, and when those gloved astronaut hands planted the first origami stars and stripes on the Moon, the whole world held its breath and watched. You, being those few years younger, don't remember it, but the way you fold the pillow cases, sharp edge to sharp edge, could have stopped paper clocks.

Half a Century

Although our eyes were fixed outside, captivated by the unchanging horizon, we both sensed that the room was shifting behind us. The worn carpet gave way to polished boards, the iron bedstead to a compact divan, and the bold floral wallpaper faded to a cool, uniform blue. Knick-knacks disappeared from the dark dresser which, in turn, gave way to clean, white drawers. We barely noticed its reflection in the window, but the sound of our breathing changed. Outside, nothing moved. Inside, our hands didn't touch.

The Do-It-Yourself Horror Movie

Occasionally, I try on strangers' hands, squeezing my fingers into their elastic skin, pinching them tight at the wrists. I like to feel how different it is playing the mandolin, how the left fingertips respond to the nip of unfamiliar strings. Other times I'll just do the washing up and see how hot I can run the water before I have to pull them out, red and dripping. Sometimes I forget I have them on, and they'll slip things into my pockets without my noticing: I'll get home to find books, watches, bars of chocolate – anything – weighing down my coat, and won't know what to do with this unwished-for loot. Generally, I'll bury it in the local park on moonless nights, and bury the hands with it so no-one will know it was me.

Space Invaders

It's like retro-gaming or gathering chestnuts, a memory tucked behind the buff envelopes on the hall table. I don't remember the rules, but there's a muscle memory to guide me, a mix of faith and reflex, like a small religion. I used to have visions – the dead and their symbols would appear at the foot of my bed, framed against the window with its thin curtains – but the walls between worlds have calcified, leaving the unborn curled on the cold pavement outside, tended by relatives I've never met. I've a box of documents – births, marriages, deaths – to which I add my degree certificates, my driving licence, my prescriptions. Trees now grow through the floor of my old room, and my ears ring with the ping and hiss of deep space.

DIY for the Unconvinced

Behind the mirror is a mirror: behind the shadow is a shadow. You lean in close to paint new layers – a face over faces, another shell to keep out the shadows – and you barely notice a small boy, red-eyed and thin: no, just thin, because he is pure monochrome, painted in shades of silver-grey. It would be easy to say he is you, to draw parallels and consequences, but you don't recognise him any more than you recognise yourself in the reflections behind reflections; his name is not your name, and when you try it on, it pinches like clothes pegs, chafes like a tiger's tongue. Behind your head is a bed; is a body that turns to the wall, that turns to sack and sawdust when you hold it, but which is always waiting for the right words, which you can never find in the mirror behind the mirror behind the mirror.

When He Leaves

When he leaves the house in the middle of the night, your swallow is louder than the closing door. By the time you have dressed, there is no sign of him, each of the three roads filled with unruffled black air, waiting like a grounded helicopter. You set your course to magnetic nowhere, walking across parks and gardens, through sleeping bedrooms and empty shops where mannequins may or may not dream. *As the crow flies*, without wings or prophecy. It's dawn before you find him on the coast, coated arms tight around absence, still as a chapel, staring down the day to see who'll blink first.

Au

As you were slight as a paper doll, I hear they could only pan 0.1 milligrams of gold from your body before they buried it, but I'm glad they made the effort. I remember how you used to stand on a chair to reach the breakfast cereal, how you'd laugh too loud and at different times to everyone else, and how your legs crossed as you sat on the floor. You were more precious than anyone gave you credit for, and I think about your children like I think about Victorian fiction, remember your lovers like the brothers whose names I can't remember from *Bonanza!* I wonder what happened to the ring I gave you. I wonder where you're buried. I wonder: what can you even do with 0.1 milligrams of gold?

In a Stranger's Car

Wounds heal eventually, but leave an area of numbness. In the back of the car, cans of Coke open themselves, ooze sticky sweetness into children's handprints, and scattered paperbacks invent new languages, each with more complex grammatical rules. I consider telling you that this afternoon I saw a human skeleton walking across the car park, flanked by black and white cats, but somehow the right opening doesn't come up, so we carry on talking about what we should and shouldn't do, an ethics of abstract hypotheses to balance the way we know things are. Let me start again: wounds never heal, and there is always an ache. I'm consciously ignoring the residue of spilt words, but they're somewhere inside; shifting shapes, growing teeth, growing fingers.

Highway Code: Addendum

We missed the turn, but your First Rule of Motorways stated that the next exit would loop us round, bring us back, and that we could make up time later. But now it is later, and we're in the dead time, the flat lands, the country without signs or shadows that we thought we'd left behind with Arthur Rackham and Edmund Dulac. After *Once upon a time* . . . anything can happen, and the figures by the way have awfully long thumbs, pricked with needles. If there were a house, we would ask for shelter, sleep with a sword between us, and breakfast on ashes; we could run away down a breadcrumb trail, with wolfbreath hot at our necks. Your Second Rule of Motorways states that names are power, that the chapman at the gate sells curses sprinkled with sugar, and that only stars are to be trusted. Windscreen wipers reveal faces in the trees, a straight road to the gingerbread house, and I consider the last of my three wishes.

Jazz

When I finally cleared the wardrobe, I found your song, crumpled on the back of an old bank statement. I didn't know how long it had been there, but it was still as clear as when you were young, your voice soft but assured, filling the room. I found a stub of pencil, and sketched in bass, piano, hi-hat and snare, a supple vamp to carry it higher. I opened the window for the first time since you left, to let waves of music break over the street, flooding the city, sweeping priests and undertakers off their feet. And there you are now, downtown, shimmying with your shopping bags, beating time with your sharp high heels.

The Beast from the East

We personify weather until it starts to speak. *Why are you here?* asks Snow, idly sculpting walls and gardens, kerbs and cars, into innocent hills. I can't answer, and feel slightly embarrassed, bumbling keys through gloves, watching my step lest I slip and snap. Snow's question nags through the day as it leans on the sill, taps at the window, politely but firmly demanding to be allowed in, sliding its fingers through the slightest crack. Last week, I read how crows have been observed using basic tools, queering species definition, or at least mocking our monopoly on evolution; and here's Snow, speaking in my own language, demanding rights, arguing the genetic toss. I apologise for windows and walls, for air conditioning. *It's ok*, says Snow, *I can wait.*

. . . to Station

So when the doors close, that's it: the end of everything, whether there's a new beginning or not. I've never made plans, and it's too late to start now, so I begin by listing my assets: credit card, debit card, £48.67 in cash, along with a few euros from a recent holiday, the clothes I'm sitting down in, all of my own teeth, a remnant of my hair, a few extra pounds I've never managed to shift and have just got used to, and a tall – maybe 2ft, or perhaps a touch more – domed cage in which is perched a canary. The train's pretty crowded, so I have to hold the cage on my lap, which means looking at the woman opposite through twinned bars. It's like she's visiting me in prison, and I wonder if she has a file in a cake, or perhaps a confession of an affair that nobody wanted to happen, but it did, and she tried to wait for me, but she couldn't, and it breaks my heart but I can't blame her, and I can't hold back my sobbing any more, and she leans forward ... She looks at the canary, and then at me, and I see that she's crying, too, and so is everyone in the carriage, and the ticket collector is weeping and handing out tissues with neat holes clipped in each corner, and the canary is singing like I've never heard before.

Cats' Eyes

On reflection, it's like astronomy or microbiology: the same patterns, the same chances. I'm not sure if it's the illness or the medication, but I need to shut my eyes on the road at night, as cats' eyes and headlights mesh into flamebirds that swoop and squabble across the windscreen. Of course, it's harder when I'm the driver, rather than just a passenger, but I find that my other senses are sharper and compensate. I navigate by the instructions of the angel on my right shoulder, careful not to be fooled by the devil on my left, who does an uncanny impersonation. A few nights ago, I accidentally took a double dose of the small pink tablets, and was forced to lean out of the car, keeping my right hand in contact with the road, and making sure I left the reek of sulphur far behind. It took all night to reach what I thought was home, and when I woke up all I could taste was the wrong person's tongue.

At the Late-Night Pharmacy

Returning unused medicines is an echo of sacrifice, a ritual of solid regret. White coated priests receive my gathered offerings with smiles, but nothing else or, perhaps, a spiritual surety so deep that it no longer ripples the surface. I wonder what they do with them. Are they added to the next communion? Or are they shelved in a vast mausoleum? *Here lie lives unsustained.* It is a maze not to be entered lightly, a labyrinth no-one wholly leaves, a blister-packed eternity in each proprietary step. But here it is raining lightly, gods are mere conjecture, and the placebos are all unconvincing.

Wrapping

Now, stitched into my old skin, I try not to burst. There are emails from foreign banks, from widows, from royalty; there are adverts for funeral cover and beautiful Russian girlfriends, but my phone's dead and no-one has sent flowers.

Acknowledgements

The poems in this collection were written as part of the Prose Poetry Project run by the International Poetry Studies Institute (IPSI) at the University of Canberra. Some of them have been published in: *Elbow Room*; *Eunoia Review*; and *Tract*, ed. Monica Carroll and Paul Munden (Recent Work Press, 2017).

This chapbook is dedicated to Amina Alyal, Miles Salter and Hannah Stone, without whose support and friendship it would almost certainly not have been written.

Oz Hardwick is a writer, photographer, music journalist, and occasional musician, based in York (UK). His work has been published and performed internationally in and on diverse media: books, journals, record covers, concert programmes, fabric, with music, with film, and with nothing but a voice. He has published six poetry collections, most recently *The House of Ghosts and Mirrors* (Valley Press, 2017), and has edited and co-edited several more. Oz is Professor of English at Leeds Trinity University, where he leads the Creative Writing programmes.

IPSI: International Poetry Studies Institute

The International Poetry Studies Institute (IPSI) is part of the Centre for Creative and Cultural Research, Faculty of Arts and Design, University of Canberra. IPSI conducts research related to poetry, and publishes and promulgates the outcomes of this research internationally. The institute also publishes poetry and interviews with poets, as well as related material, from around the world. Publication of such material takes place in IPSI's online journal *Axon: Creative Explorations* (www. axonjournal.com.au) and through other publishing vehicles, such as Axon Elements. IPSI's goals include working – collaboratively, where possible – for the appreciation and understanding of poetry, poetic language and the cultural and social significance of poetry. The institute also organises symposia, seminars, readings and other poetry-related activities and events.

IPSI Chapbook Series

The IPSI Chapbook Series publishes new work by leading poets from Australia and beyond, in limited editions. The chapbooks feature extended selections beyond the scope of most journals, highlighting innovative work by poets both new and well established, ahead of publication in book form. The series is linked to an international program of poets in residence at the University of Canberra.
Series Editor: Paul Munden.

CCCR: Centre for Creative & Cultural Research

The Centre for Creative and Cultural Research (CCCR) is IPSI's umbrella organisation and brings together staff, adjuncts, research students and visiting fellows who work on key challenges within the cultural sector and creative field. A central feature of its research concerns the effects of digitisation and globalisation on cultural producers, whether individuals, communities or organisations.